Clara's Traveling Piano

Based on a true story by
ANN MAGEE

Illustrated by
PAUL SCHULTZ

FriesenPress

One Printers Way
Altona, MB R0G 0B0
Canada

www.friesenpress.com

Copyright © 2025 by Ann Magee
First Edition — 2025

Cover and Interior Illustrations by Paul Schultz

All rights reserved.

No part of this publication may be reproduced in any form, or by any means, electronic or mechanical, including photocopying, recording, or any information browsing, storage, or retrieval system, without permission in writing from FriesenPress.

**Authors proceeds will be given to the
David Foster Foundation
To help support families with children who need
lifesaving organ transplants**

ISBN
978-1-03-830652-4 (Hardcover)
978-1-03-830651-7 (Paperback)
978-1-03-830653-1 (eBook)

1. JUVENILE NONFICTION, FAMILY

Distributed to the trade by The Ingram Book Company

Dedicated

to my five grandchildren

Who inspired me to write
this book

Henry, Samuel, Rosemary,
Harvey and Wesley

Our story begins in
Milwaukee Wisconsin 1920

There lived a little girl named Clara.
Clara wanted to learn to

PLAY THE PIANO.

So Clara's parents enrolled
her in piano lessons.

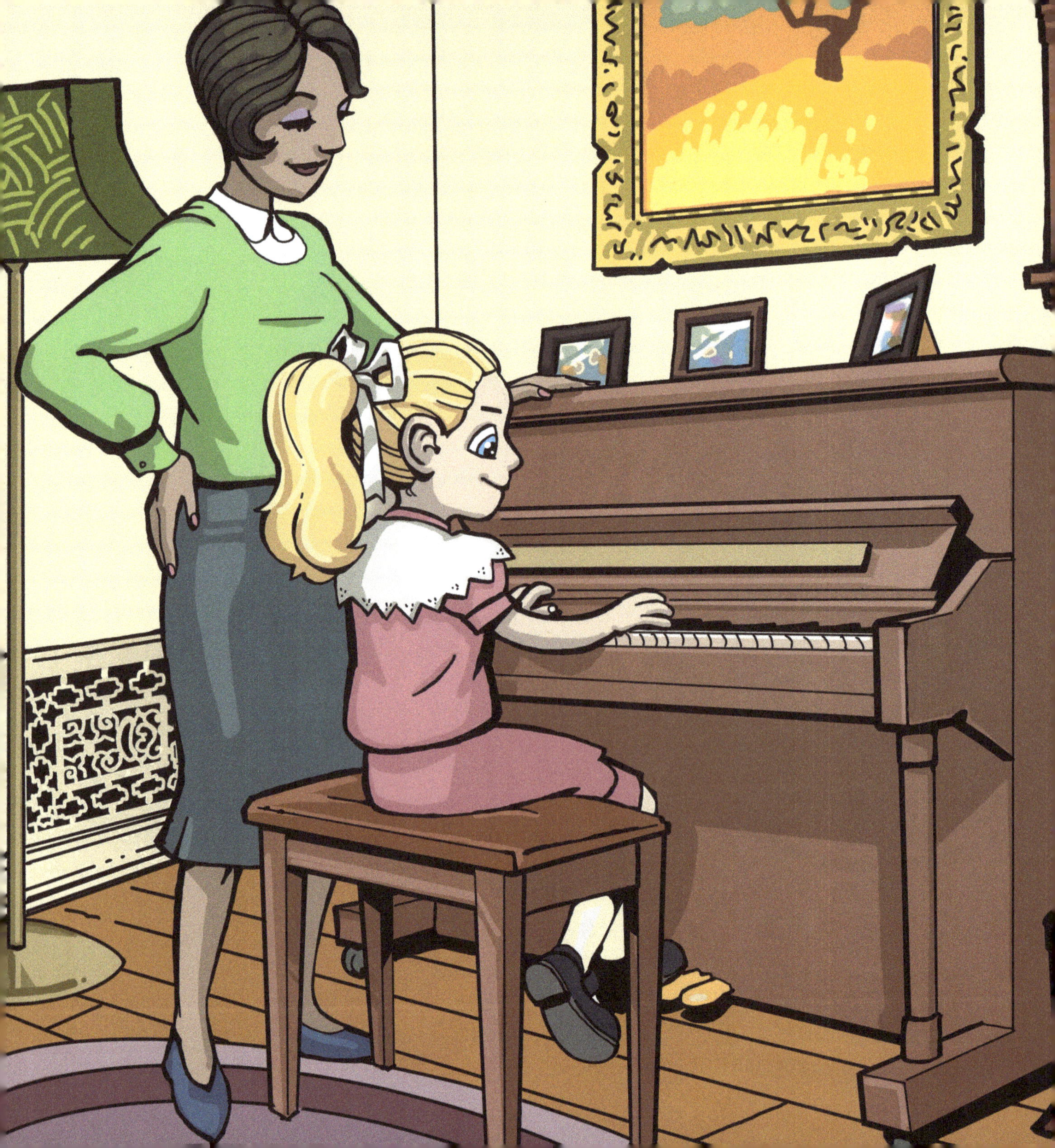

Clara
LOVED HER LESSONS

and wanted to play more,
but they did not have a piano
at home so she could only
play when she was at the
teacher's house.

After a while, Clara's parents saw how committed Clara was to playing the piano, so when she was fourteen years old they bought her a

BEAUTIFUL PIANO!

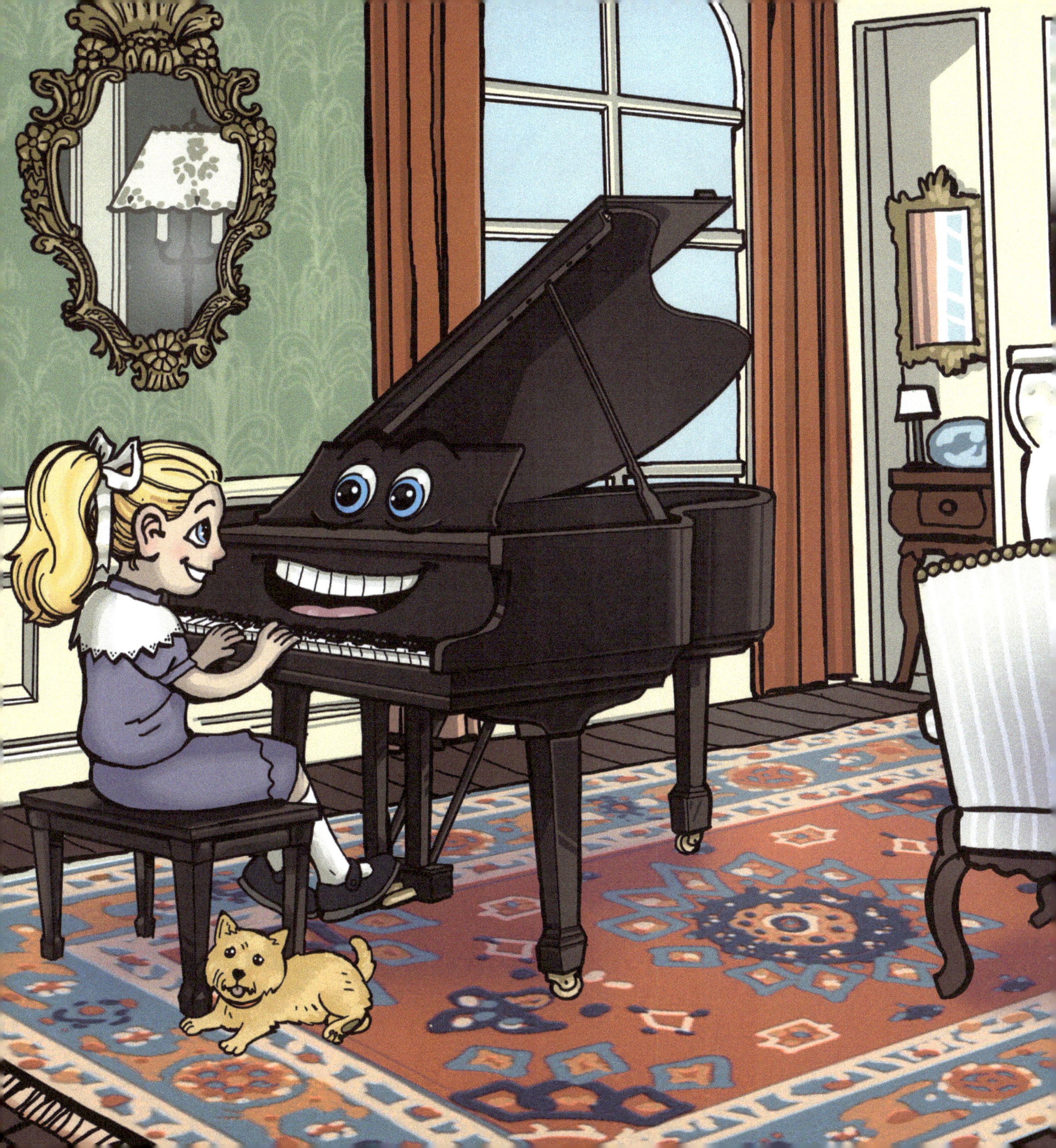

Clara loved her

PIANO

and practiced every day.

Clara played and played for many years.

One day Clara got married and took her beloved

PIANO

to her new home.

Clara and her husband, Allan, had two boys.

John the eldest loved to play Piano, but James did not, he would rather play football,

and that's ok too but his mother still wanted him to take lessons, but he did not like them!

John continued to PLAY
on Clara's Piano
until he left home for university,
but James had quit his lessons a long time back.

After the boys were gone, it was just Clara that was left playing her

BELOVED PIANO.

But over time, Clara got very old and could no longer play her Piano.

Clara had to move to a nursing home and sadly Piano could not go with her.

PIANO MISSED CLARA
SO MUCH!

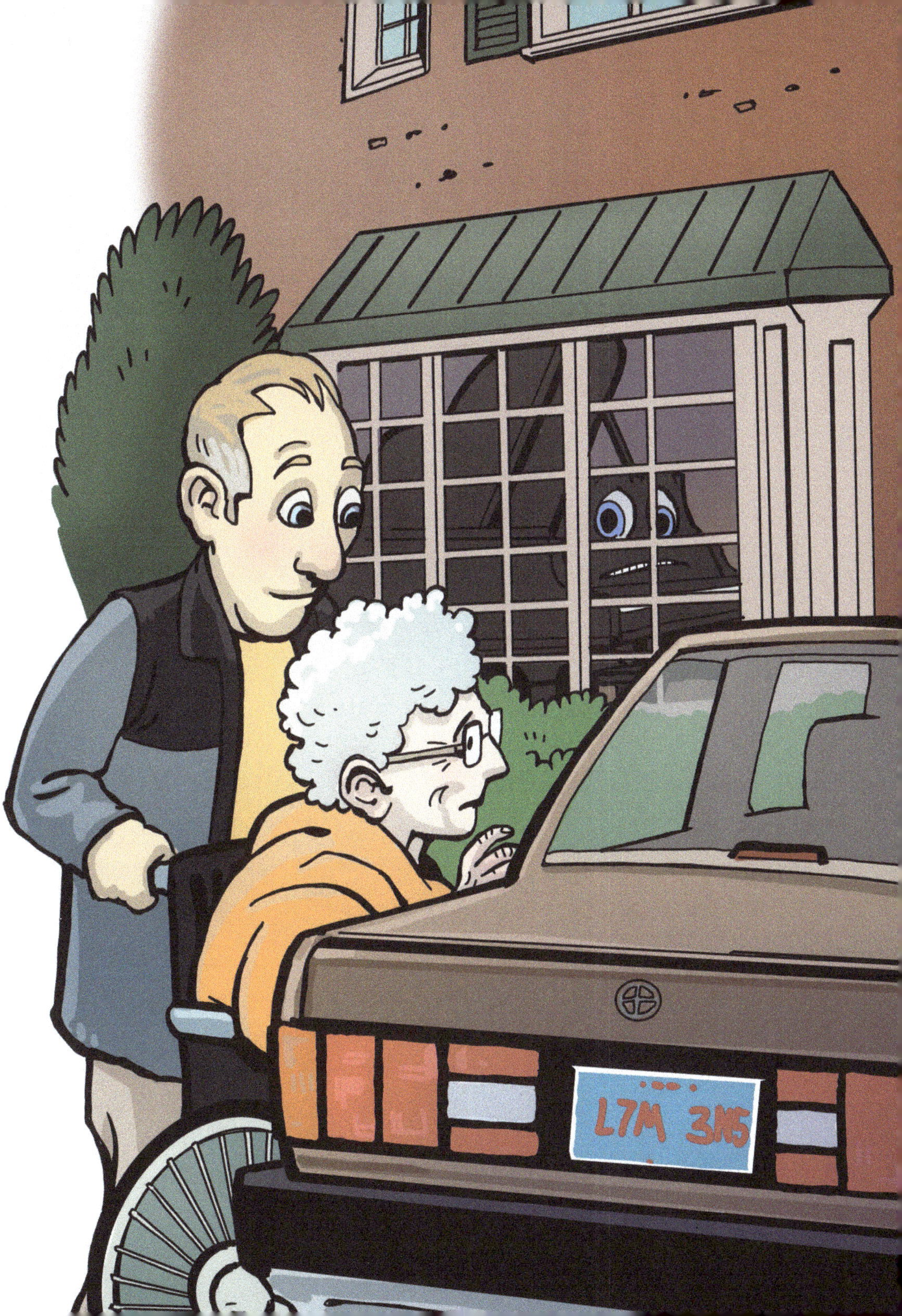
L7M 3N5

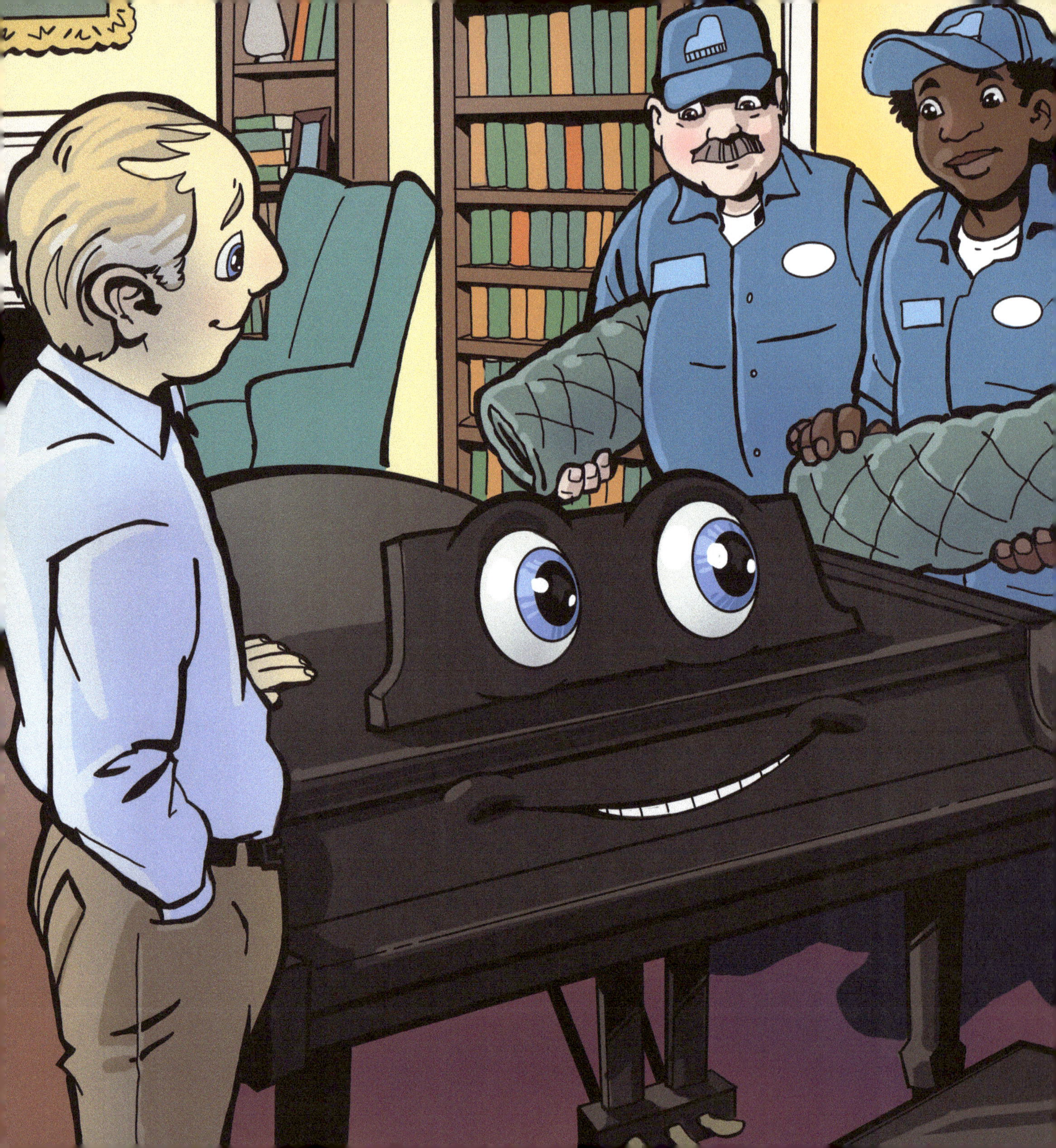

John could not take his mother's Piano as he had moved all the way to Asia!

Clara's son James, who now lived in Pasadena, California, said he would move Piano to his house. He hoped his two little girls, Caroline and Margaret, would

PLAY CLARA'S PIANO.

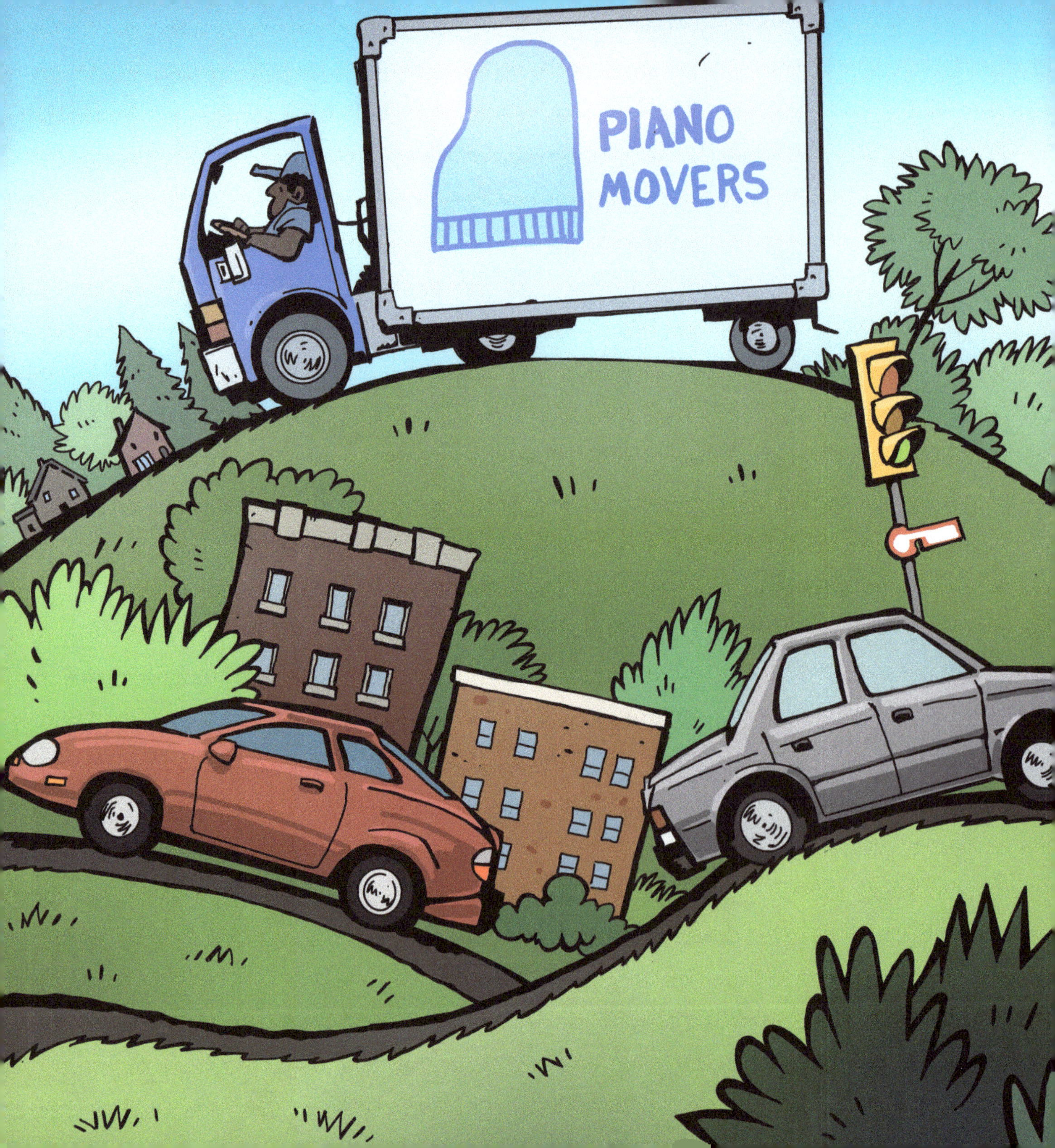
PIANO
MOVERS

So Clara's Piano was carefully wrapped and put in a special truck and travelled

2,467 MILES

to go all the way to Pasadena, California from Milwaukee, Wisconsin.

Piano was so looking forward to a new home!

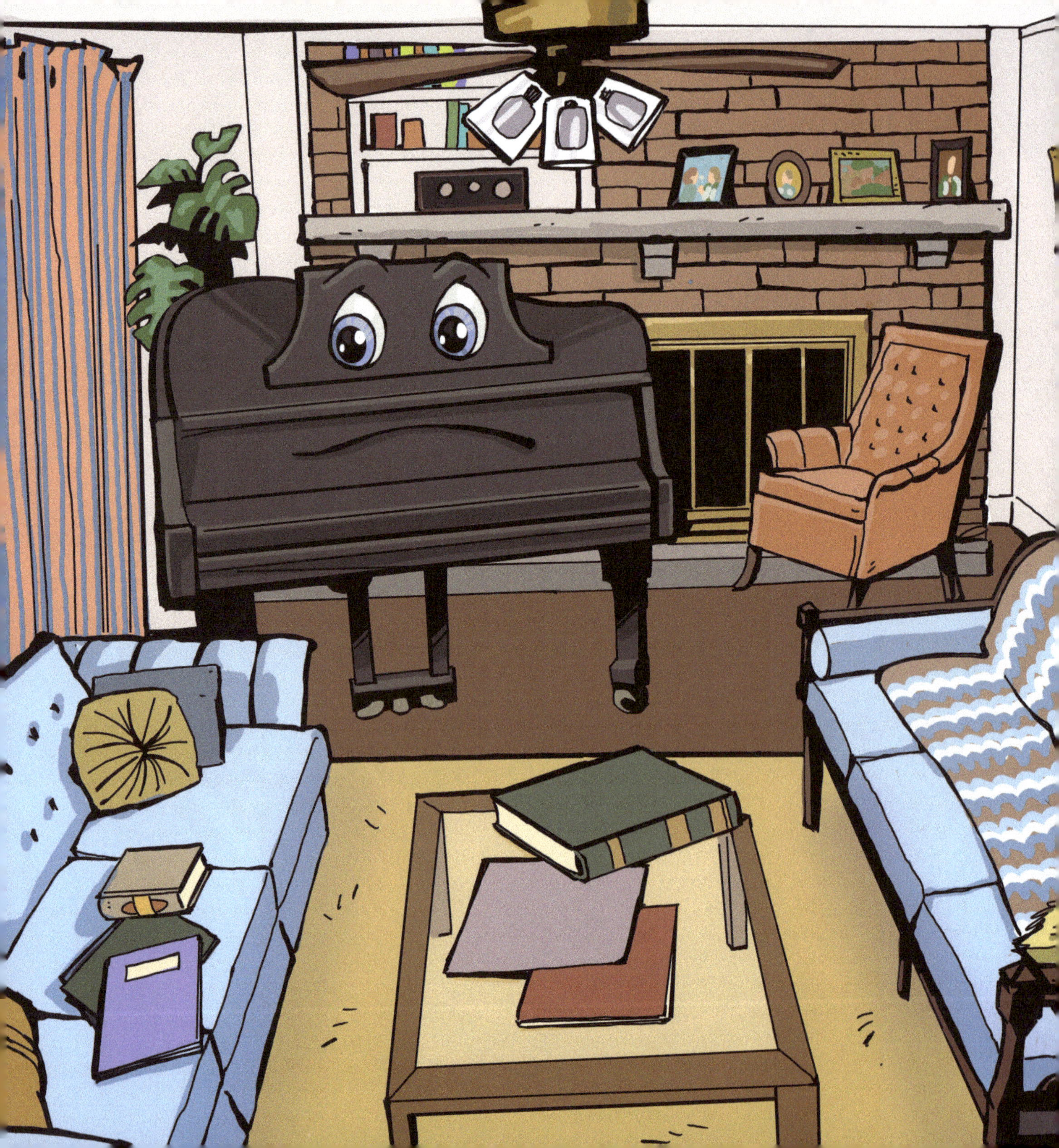

James daughters took lessons,
but they did not love to play like Clara did.

They wanted to do other things.

So, Clara's beautiful Piano
SAT ALL ALONE
in the lovely living room.

PIANO WAS SAD, ONCE AGAIN.

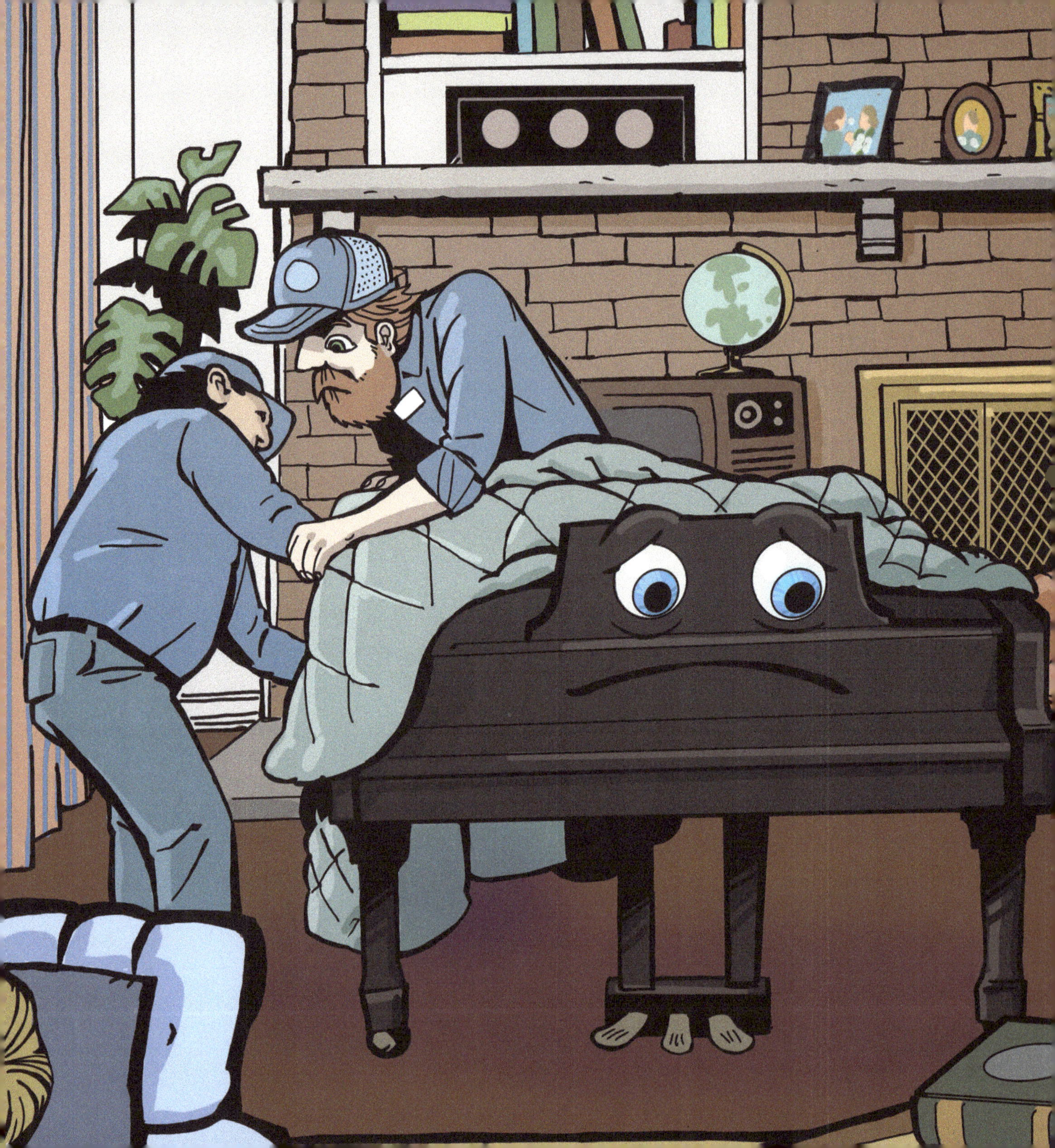

One day James and his wife decided
Piano was taking up

TOO MUCH SPACE

in their living room.

As no one was playing it,
they decided to put

PIANO

into a storage unit near their house.

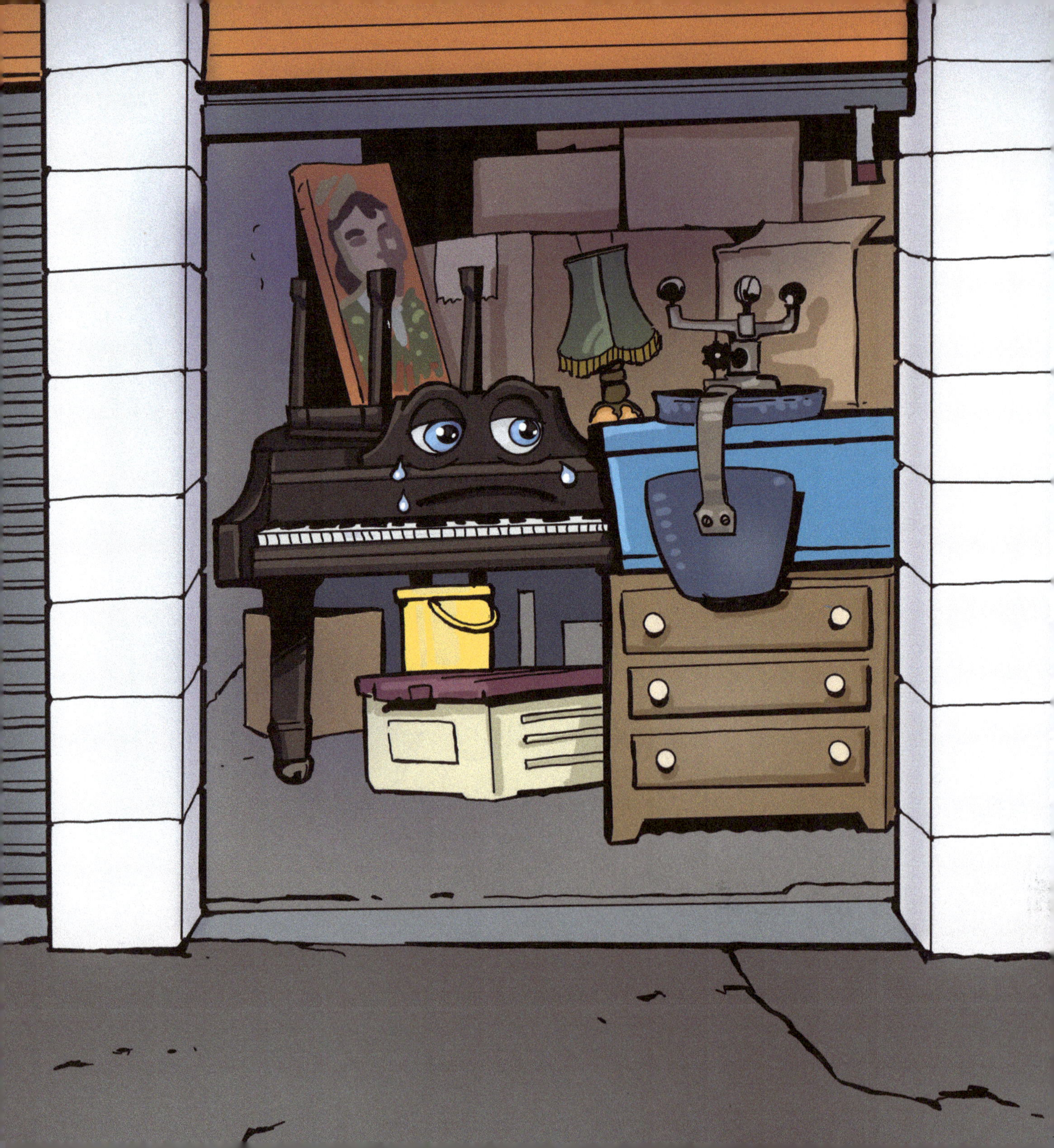

So once again, Piano was carefully
wrapped up and moved away.

POOR CLARA'S PIANO!

Stuck in a storage unit with so many other
unloved and forgotten possessions.

LEFT THERE TO BE FORGOTTEN!

Piano got very dusty and badly out of tune.

Would Piano ever get played again?

Piano was very upset!

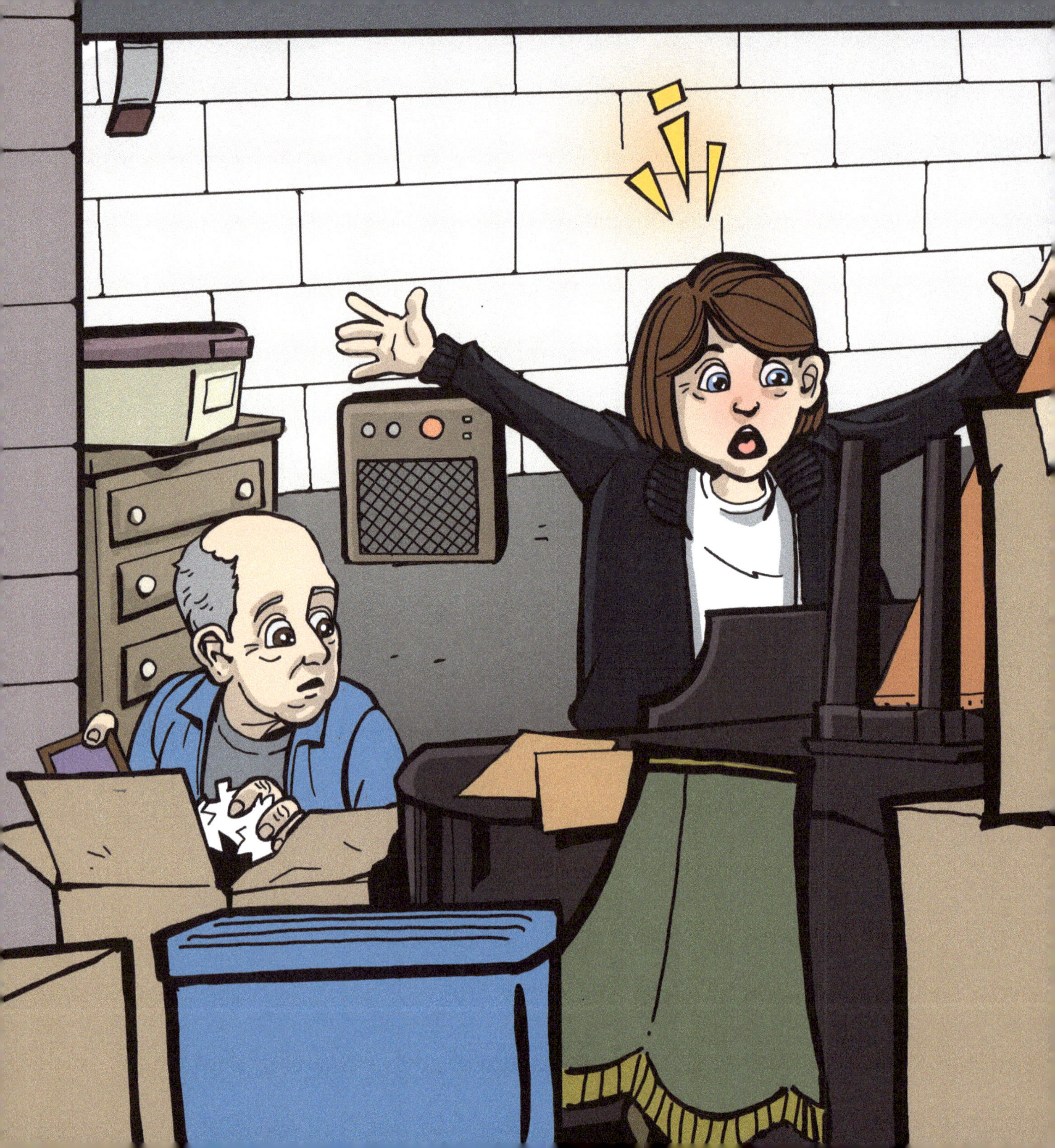

After many years, James and his new wife Ann went to the storage unit to look for some things that James wanted.

Ann spotted the **BEAUTIFUL**, but now **OLD** and **SAD**, Piano and said, " you have to save this Piano! Get it out of here!"

So James decided to send **PIANO** once again on another journey.

This time to Atlanta, Georgia,

2,164 MILES

away where his three grandchilden,
Clara, Cullen and John would surely play Piano!

Piano was carefully wrapped and put in a truck to begin another adventure.

Piano was very excited!

But when they got to Piano's new home, there was no room for it, so they put Piano downstairs in the basement with all the other leftover things.

Piano felt like it was back in storage again!

UGH!!!!

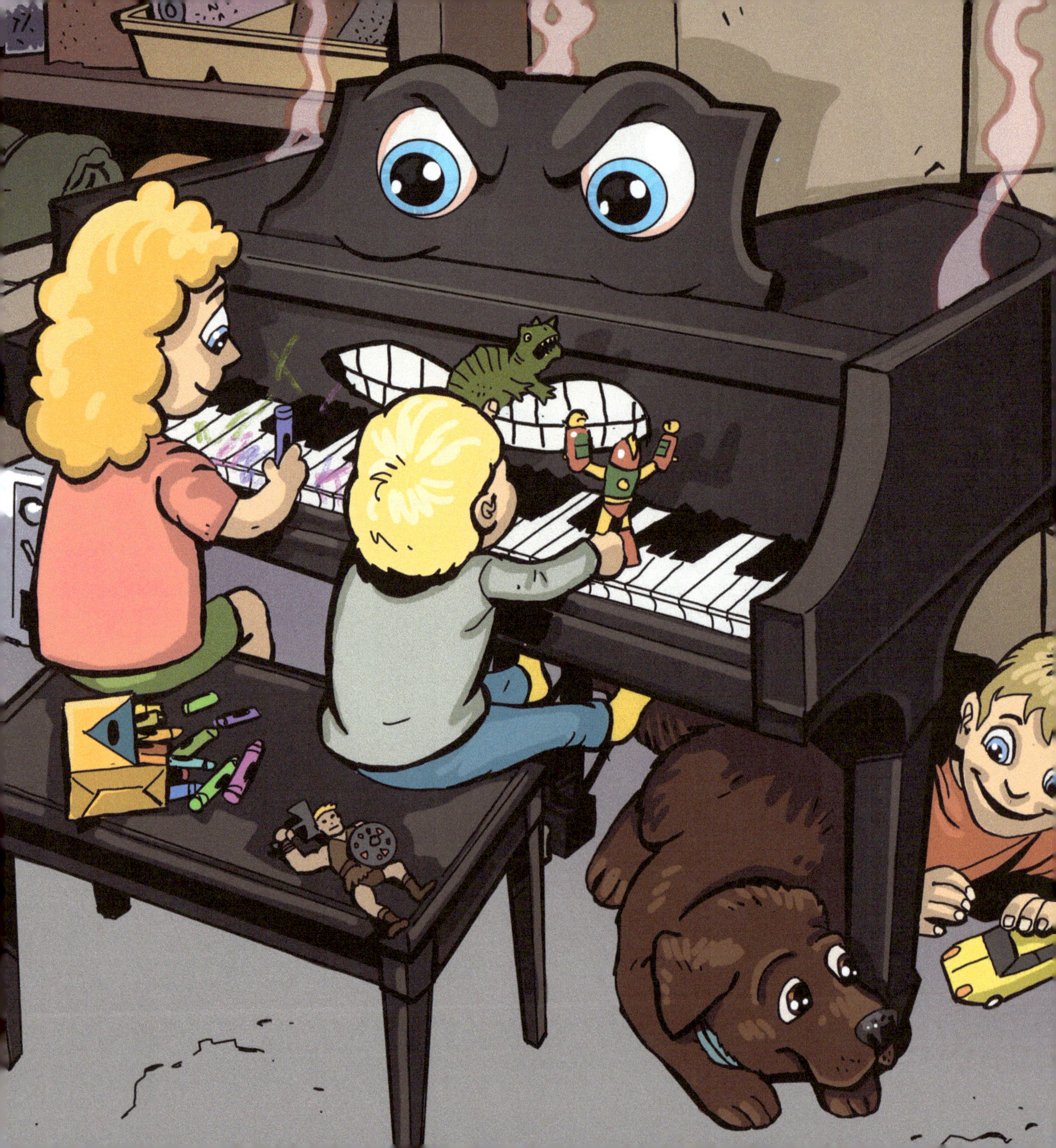

Sometimes the children would go
down and play with Piano,

but they also thought
it was fun to color on the
beautiful ivory keys.

THIS MADE PIANO
VERY ANGRY!

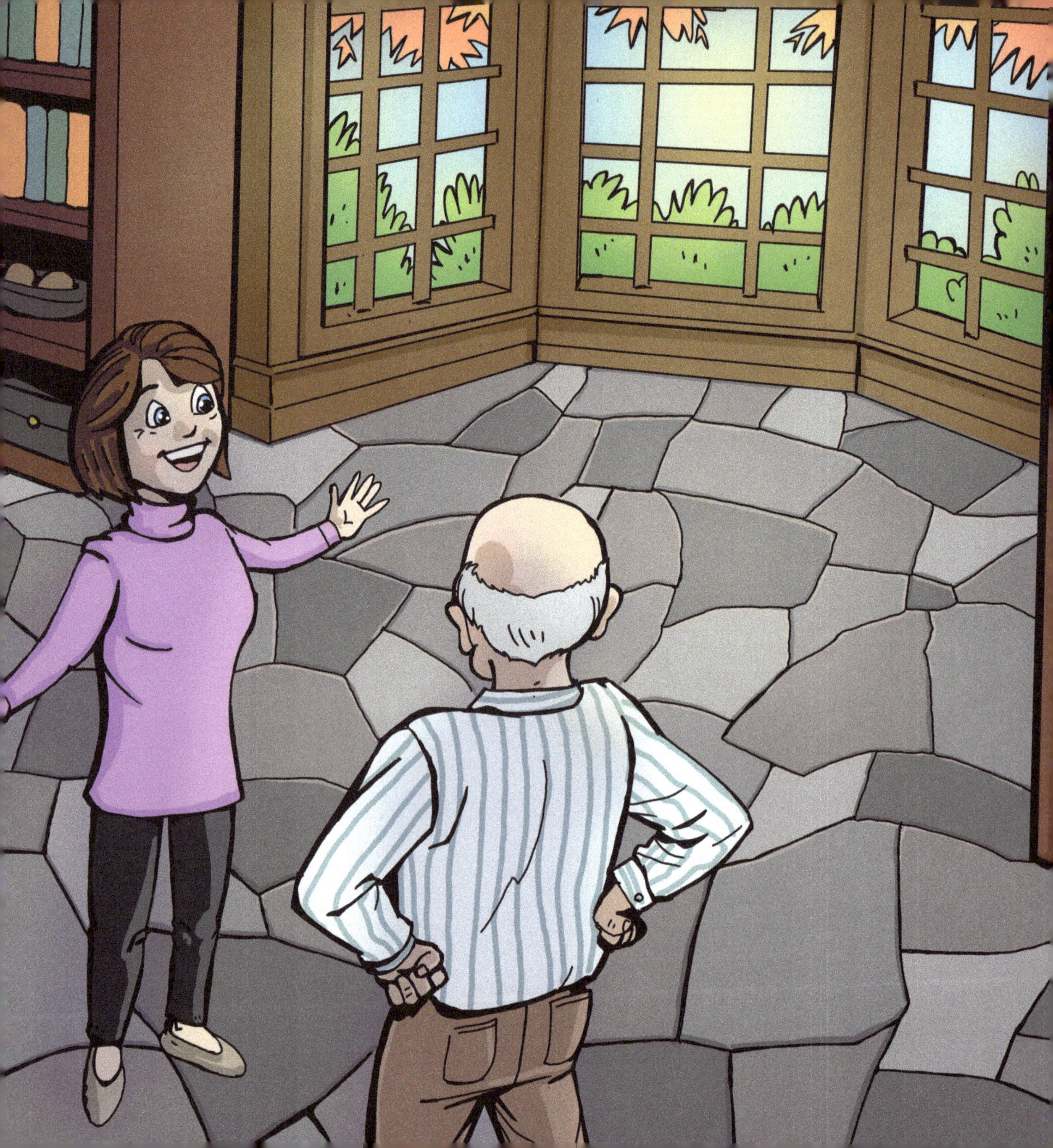

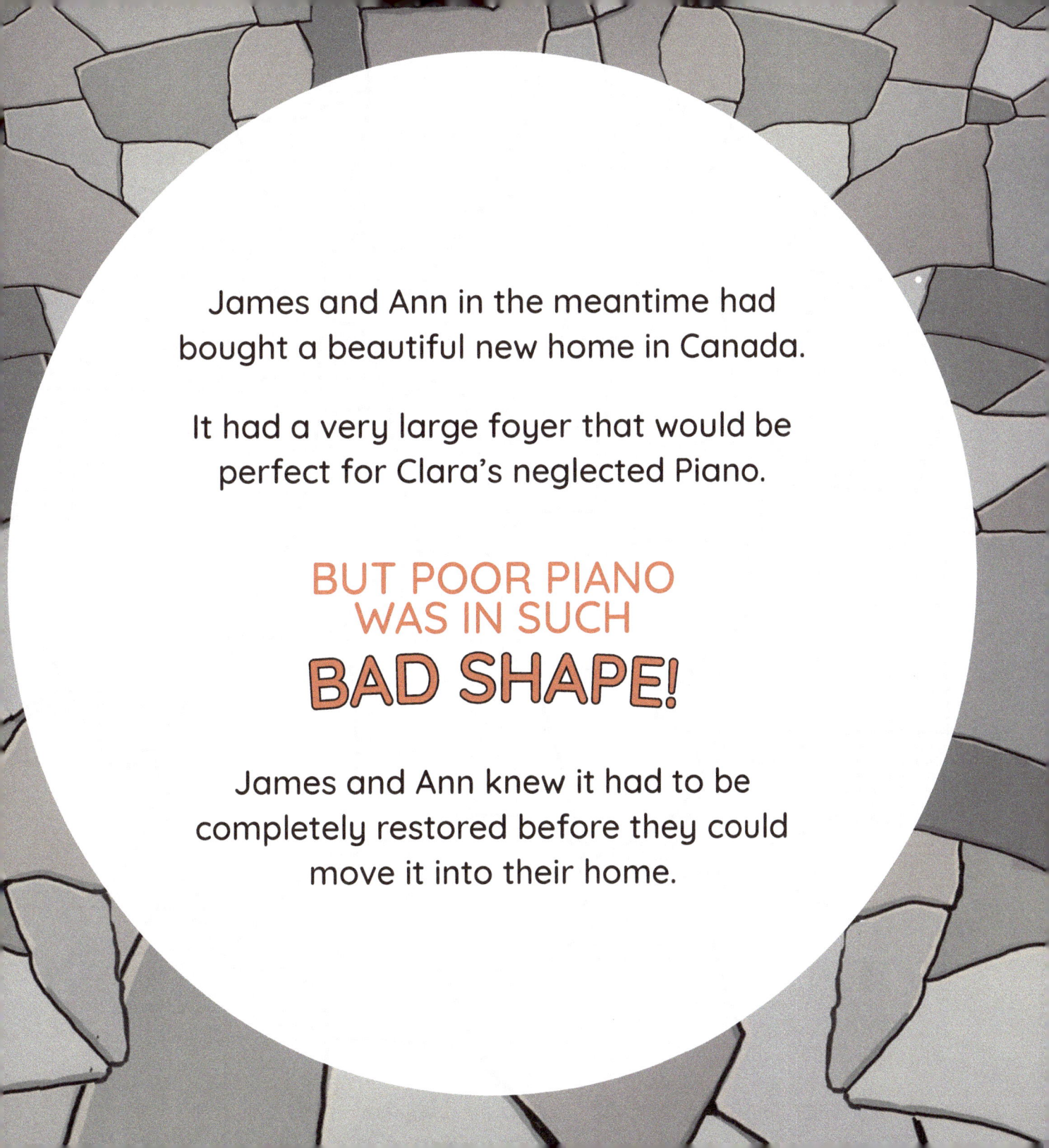

James and Ann in the meantime had bought a beautiful new home in Canada.

It had a very large foyer that would be perfect for Clara's neglected Piano.

BUT POOR PIANO WAS IN SUCH BAD SHAPE!

James and Ann knew it had to be completely restored before they could move it into their home.

So once again Piano was carefully wrapped up and put in a truck and sent all the way to Pine Brook, New Jersey

805 MILES
away.

When it arrived at the restoration factory, Clara's Piano was lovingly taken apart and after many months was restored back to it's original beauty and sound.

Piano had not been this HAPPY in years!

Clara's beloved Piano once again, was wrapped up, and carefully put on a special truck and taken this time, all the way to Canada to Ann and James home in Caledon, Ontario

493 MILES away.

Upon arrival, Piano was lovingly unwrapped and placed carefully by the window in their beautiful foyer.

After many years Piano was tuned and ready to be played once again!

PIANO WAS THRILLED!

But who is going to play Piano?

Well, to everyone's surprise, James admitted that he regretted not listening to his mother about continuing his piano lessons.

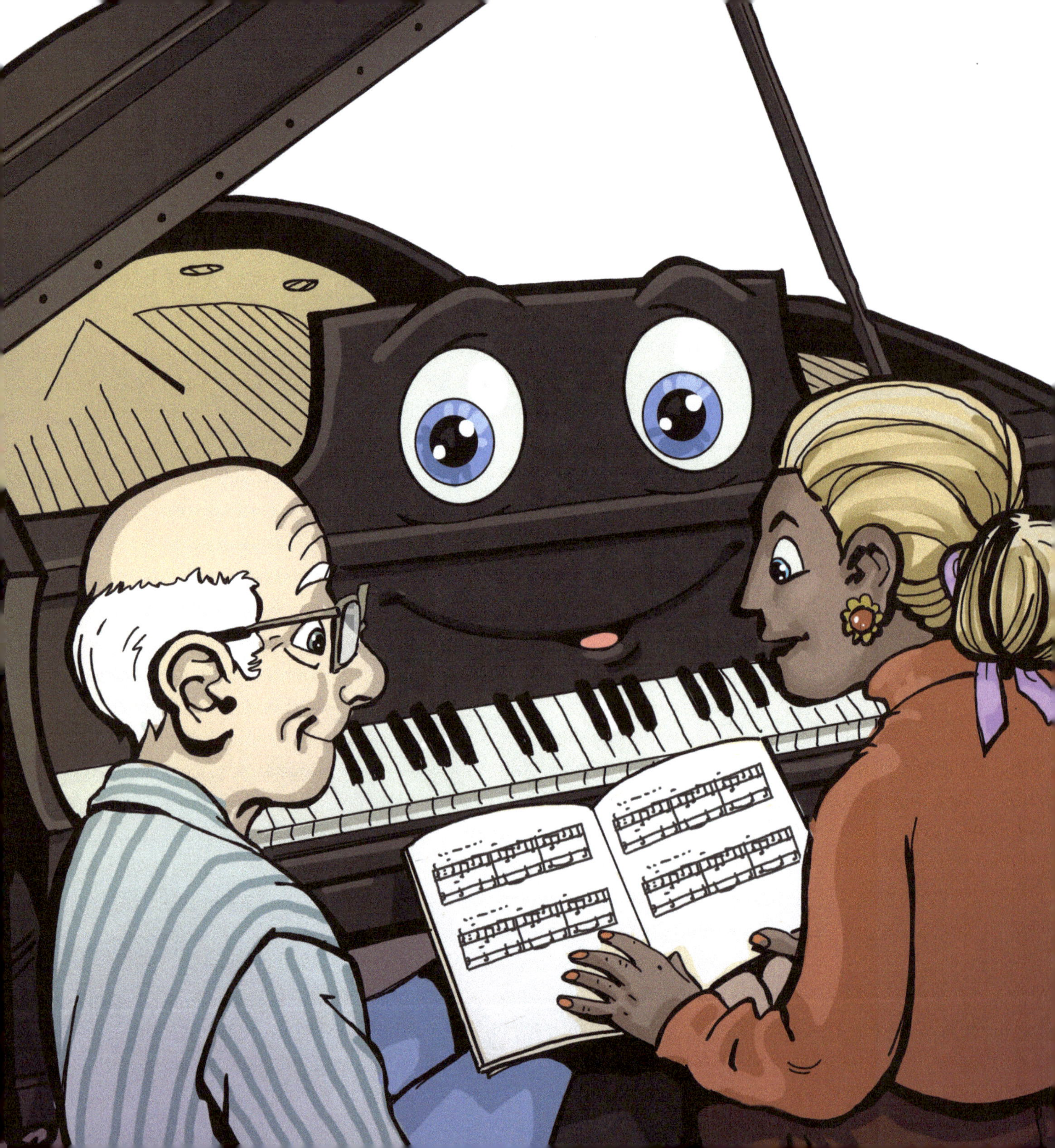

So, James found a teacher
and is finally learning to play
the piano
after all these years

AND THIS MAKES PIANO VERY HAPPY!

CANADA
Ontario
Caledon
Wisconsin
California
Milwaukee
Pine
Brook
New Jers
USA
Pasadena
Atlanta
Georgia

And just in case you were wondering,
Clara's piano travelled

5,929 MILES
FROM 1920 – 2018

97 YEARS!